THE
Archive Photographs
SERIES

INDUSTRIES
OF
WALES

Compiled by
William Troughton,
from the collection of the National Library of Wales

CHALFORD

First published 1997
Copyright © The National Library of Wales, 1997

The Chalford Publishing Company
St Mary's Mill, Chalford,
Stroud, Gloucestershire, GL6 8NX

ISBN 0 7524 1070 9

Typesetting and origination by
The Chalford Publishing Company
Printed in Great Britain by
Bailey Print, Dursley, Gloucestershire

THE
Archive Photographs
SERIES

INDUSTRIES
OF
WALES

Contents

Pentre Ceramic Works, Acre-fair, 1955. Brick and tile making has long been associated with the Ruabon area near Wrexham. During the post-war years this company's products were much in demand for re-building Blitz-damaged London.

Introduction

Since the National Library of Wales was granted a Royal Charter in 1907 generations of staff have assiduously built up the collections of books, manuscripts, maps, pictures and, by no means least, photographs. This collection now totals in excess of 600,000 photographs covering numerous aspects of life in Wales. The collection includes the earliest-known photograph of Wales – a daguerreotype of Margam Castle dating from 1841. Acquisition of works by the most noteworthy contemporary photographers working in Wales today keeps the collection up to date and reflects the constant evolution of our society.

The images chosen for this book represent the work of many photographers, some professional, others talented amateurs. Amongst the earliest photographs reproduced here are those by John Thomas. His business premises was in Liverpool but from the 1860s until the 1890s he spent much of his time travelling around Wales with his horse-drawn darkroom taking portraits of ordinary people, very often at their workplaces. Other photographers, although professional, derived their income from the immediate area in which they lived. D.C. Harries, for example, maintained studios in Llandeilo and Ammanford. The images of Pantyffynnon Colliery are from a collection of his negatives donated to the National Library after his death.

Other series of photographs were commissioned by the companies themselves. It is from this category that the photos of the Cambrian Collieries and the Clayton Tinplate Works come. The foresight of the management of these concerns cannot be too highly commended as they record ways of life long passed.

Many of the illustrations are from postcards. Often produced the same day to record a notable event, postcards often had an impact and role similar to the newspaper photographs of today. They were used to illustrate all aspects of Edwardian Britain. Apart from the cards of Senghenydd discussed in the text, perhaps the most noteworthy are the underground scenes taken by Pentre photographer Stephen Timothy. The use of flash photography underground, even in mines regarded as being free of gas, was still a potentially dangerous task at the time Timothy worked.

Another photographer who travelled Wales with his camera, but without a need for a portable darkroom, was Geoff Charles. Trained as a journalist, Charles began taking photographs to illustrate his news stories. In a career that spanned forty years he took over 120,000 photographs illustrating all aspects of life in Wales and became the principality's leading photojournalist. His photos of quarries, factories and steelworks all show the human side of these industries.

The photographic collection continues to grow at a rapid pace. It is hoped that this selection of images, focusing on one aspect of Welsh life, will draw attention to the many fine photographs in the collection which can be viewed at the National Library of Wales in Aberystwyth.

Quarryman, *c.* 1910. The numbers of both industrial injuries and horses have declined markedly as this century has progressed. Industry today is a far safer place to work.

One

Docks and Dock Industries

The need to import raw materials and export finished products from the copper and iron industries led to a thriving sea trade from the moment these industries started. Loading and unloading was conducted from wharves alongside rivers such as the Taff, Tawe and Afan although these had the disadvantage of relying on the tide for access. As ships got bigger, and trade, especially in sale coal increased, so the need for better facilities became apparent. Docks capable of loading and unloading at any state of the tide were built at Port Talbot in 1837, in Cardiff (West Bute Dock) in 1839 and Swansea (North Dock) in 1844. Newport made do with the River Usk until a small dock of 4.5 acres, later expanded, was built in 1842. The 28.5-acre Alexandra Dock was completed in 1875. Barry Docks were built as a result of the congestion, delays and high charges that were a feature of Cardiff Docks. The Marquess of Bute owned both the Taff Vale Railway and the port. Despite earlier promises to improve and expand the port facilities he took no action until 1882 when he threatened to increase the shipping charges levied on coal-owners. As a result interested parties decided to build their own docks, subsequently deciding on Barry as a suitable site. A leading campaigner for the construction of docks at Barry was David Davies of Llandinam, owner of the Ocean Collieries. He and his consortium obtained Parliamentary approval to build docks at Barry in 1884 and the first dock was opened in 1889, followed by a second in 1898.

In 1913 the South Wales ports handled 47 million tons of exports, of which 40 million were coal. By 1938 the amount of coal exported had fallen to 19.5 million tons, and in 1969 the figure was a meagre 1.75 million tons, most of which was exported through Swansea.

Today Cardiff and Barry Docks are run by Associated British Ports. Cardiff exports approximately 50,000 tons of coal a year. Its other main export is grain. Imports include oil products and coking coal, the latter from the USA. Much of Barry's trade revolves around the importation of fruit and vegetables, especially bananas, and dry bulk goods such as cement.

In addition to the ports traditionally associated with the coal industry, Wales also has ferry ports from which regular services operate to Ireland. The foremost of these are Holyhead and Fishguard. Holyhead gained in popularity as a port after Thomas Telford built the Menai Suspension bridge and improved the road across Anglesey to Holyhead in the 1820s. The arrival of the railway in 1848 proved an even greater spur to development as it enabled travellers to reach Dublin more quickly using the Royal Mail steamers. As more passengers started to use Holyhead so the ships grew in size and comfort. This meant the harbour had to be expanded and a large quay built to protect vessels at anchor. This took 28 years to complete and was finished in 1873. In addition, the inner harbour was dredged to accommodate larger vessels and the Station Hotel was built.

Fishguard, like Holyhead, owed its status as a ferry port to the railway. The harbour was built by the Great Western Railway and officially opened in 1906. It had been the hope of the developers that transatlantic liners would be persuaded to call at Fishguard. However, despite a visit by the Mauretania in 1909 Southampton and Liverpool retained their custom. All ferries from Fishguard now run to Rosslare and include the Felicity which is capable of carrying 2,000 passengers and over 500 cars, making her the largest ferry to have sailed on any route between Britain and Ireland.

Barry Dock

Barry Dock, c. 1910. This is the first dock which was built at Barry. In the foreground are four cranes being used to unload pit props. The cranes are mounted on rails so that they can be moved along the quayside. The railway wagons on the quayside suggest that these pit props are for one of the Powell Duffryn collieries. The large building in the centre of the view is the Dock Offices. The channel to its right leads to the Barry Graving Dock.

New Dock, Barry Dock, *c.* 1910. The towers on the left are coal hoists for conveying the coal from the wagons to the ship's hold via a chute. Teams of coal trimmers were then employed to ensure that the coal was properly stowed. The large building on the centre-right is the Rank Flour Mill, built in 1906 to store wheat imported from North America.

The Dry Dock, Barry Dock

The Dry Dock, Barry Dock, *c.* 1910. The Graving Dry Dock was owned by the Barry Railway Company and opened in 1893. It was used to repair and maintain visiting ships such as the *Hans Menzell*, a German-registered vessel. It ceased to be a dry dock in 1983.

SS Walkure, 1908. Life in a busy port was never without incident as when SS *Walkure*, heavily leaden with timber destined for South Africa, developed a list while loading with coal. Despite the dramatic scene no-one was hurt and the ship later went on her way.

South Dock, Swansea, *c.* 1900. Most of these sailing vessels would have been involved in the copper trade, taking coal to South American coaling stations and returning to Swansea with either copper ore or 'regulus' (a form of semi-refined copper ore). South Dock was finally closed in 1972 and subsequently filled in.

The Docks, Port Talbot, *c*. 1912. Port Talbot Docks were used both for the export of coal and the import of iron ore for the local steelworks. Coal hoists can be seen on both left and right. These docks were closed in 1972 after a new 500-acre dock was opened able to handle 100,000-ton iron-ore vessels.

Docks, Port Talbot, *c*. 1905. Included here is the *Castleton*, a three-masted vessel of 1,970 tons built at Glasgow in 1903. She was later sold to Norwegian owners and re-named *Svalen*.

Cardiff, The Docks, *c.* 1900. Leaving West Bute Dock, Cardiff is one of the nineteen steam trawlers owned by Neale & West, and based there. The sail on the left, marked 'Cf', belongs to a pilot cutter. Pilots were needed to guide ships the last few miles into a port as coastal waters were subject to changing conditions. The Welsh Industrial and Maritime Museum is today on the centre-right.

M.V. "CAMBRIA" (DISPLACEMENT 5000 TONS) IN HARBOUR, HOLYHEAD.   W.3300.

MV *Cambria*, *c.* 1921. The *Cambria* was owned by the London & North Western Railway and came into service at Holyhead in 1921. On arrival the mail would be passed straight to the train on the adjacent platform and rushed to London, sorting taking place en route.

14

Breakwater, Fishguard, *c.* 1907. The breakwater across the entrance to Fishguard Bay is over half a mile long and the water along most of its length is 16 metres deep. Over 2,400 tons of rock were used for every metre of length of the breakwater. The rock required came from the area in the foreground now occupied by the station.

Fishguard. Landing Stage, *c.* 1907. The proximity of the harbour station to the quayside and the extensive railway sheds made it easy for both passengers and goods to be transferred to the railway. The *Inniscarra*, owned by the City of Cork Steam Packet Co., can be seen moored along the quayside. She was the first vessel to officially use the new harbour.

60719. Portmadoc; Harbour.   FRITH

Porthmadog, *c*. 1900. This was one of many small ports through which slates were exported up until the outbreak of the First World War. The port owes both its creation and name to William Alexander Madocks who built the embankment known as the 'Cob' in 1825. This was done with the intention of draining the marshland behind. The project proved a success and the scour created by the diverted Glaslyn and Dwyryd rivers, which flow under the bridge in the foreground, excavated a sheltered harbour. Slate was brought down from Blaenau Ffestiniog by boat until 1836 when the Ffestiniog Railway was built. To facilitate the loading of slates on to ships increasing both in number and size the quarry-owners built quays for which they paid the Madocks estate a rental. The export of slate from Porthmadog had a number of peaks and troughs but was eventually killed off by the First World War.

On the right-hand side of the picture two sailing ships typical of the vessels that exported slates to places across Europe and even farther afield are moored at Matthews Wharf. Piles of slates from the Oakeley Quarries are on the quayside waiting to be loaded. Further downstream is Greaves Wharf which handled exports from the Llechwedd Quarry. The long huts on the left-hand side of the postcard belonged to the Welsh Slate Company.

Two

Slate

North Wales slate was used by the Romans for roofing as far back as the third century. During the eighteenth century the industry was highly fragmented with many small quarries to be found where the slate outcropped near the surface and only a few larger concerns such as Penrhyn and Nantlle. As the slate became increasingly difficult to reach and as demand increased, due in part to the Industrial Revolution, small quarries amalgamated into larger concerns. In addition, the repeal of a tax on all slates sent by sea in 1831 proved a great spur to investment in the industry. Thus it was in the last century that the industry was at its most prosperous and became indelibly linked with the history and culture of North Wales.

The industry became established in four main areas, each with its own characteristics. The first was the area around Corwen and Llangollen where the grey-blue-coloured Silurian slate was quarried, principally for use as slabs and flagstones rather than for roofing. Around Corris, Silurian slate was quarried but its qualities made some suitable for roofing while other outcrops were best suited for use as slabs for snooker tables, gravestones, window sills, vats for brewing beer and, later on, for circuit boards in the electricity industry. The third area is around Blaenau Ffestiniog where good-quality Ordovician slate with a distinct blue-grey colour is found. Much of this slate is mined underground rather than quarried from a hillside or pit. One of the best-known underground mines was the Oakeley Quarry, now better known as Gloddfa Ganol. The Blaenau Ffestiniog slate is less brittle than its counterparts elsewhere and is easier to cut with machines. The fourth and by far the most important area is in central Gwynedd, around Bethesda and Llanberis. It is in this area that slate for roofing was extracted from quarries such as Penrhyn, Dinorwig and Nantlle.

Although slate is to be found in other areas of Britain, notably Cornwall, Cumbria and parts of Scotland the best-quality slate was always that from Wales. In 1882 a total of 494,100 tons of slate was produced in Britain. Of this 92 per cent came from Wales, with the Penrhyn and Dinorwig quarries being the biggest individual contributors. Slate production reached its peak in 1898 when a total of 16,766 men were employed in the industry in North Wales and market share stood at 70 per cent.

After this date the industry suffered a series of strikes at some of the major quarries, such as

Llechwedd in 1897, culminating in the three-year lockout from 1900-03 at the Penrhyn Quarry. This proved disastrous for the industry as cheaper imports and alternatives to slate as a roofing material gained a foothold in the market place. At the time Penrhyn was producing a quarter of all Welsh slate. The First World War also did much to harm the industry as house building almost ceased, quarrymen were conscripted into the forces and the German demand for slates disappeared. The export of slate to Germany had provided an important market since a fire destroyed the city of Hamburg in 1842. Despite a building boom in the years following the war, Welsh slate failed to compete against slate from other areas of Britain and cheap imports from Belgium, France, Germany, Italy, Norway and, particularly, America. By 1939 the industry employed only 7,589 men at 41 quarries. By 1945 the figure had shrunk to 3,520 at 18 sites and in 1972 less than a thousand men were employed in the industry. Although the predominant use of slate is still as a roofing material, today it has only about 5 per cent of the British roofing trade.

The slate industry continued to decline until the 1950s. Since then it has made a partial recovery. Penrhyn Quarry is now owned by McAlpines who have been able to invest sufficient capital in the quarry to make it a viable concern. Llechwedd is still a working quarry, though, like many others, it is more famous as a tourist attraction.

The Oakeley Quarry (Gloddfa Ganol), the largest slate mine (as opposed to quarry) in the world with over 50 miles of underground railways, closed in 1971. Slate left as supporting pillars by earlier generations is now being commercially extracted.

Apart from the quarries themselves one of the most obvious legacies of the industry are the numerous narrow-gauge railways to be found in North Wales, many of which are popular tourist attractions. These often had their origins in horse-drawn tramways linking the quarries to ports such as Porthmadog, Y Felinheli and Caernarfon. The first steam locomotives were introduced in 1840 on the line from Penrhyn Quarry to Port Penrhyn. The famous Ffestiniog Railway linking Blaenau Ffestiniog to Porthmadog was built in 1869. These ports, themselves a by-product of the slate industry, in turn spawned new industries such as shipbuilding.

As well as being one of the largest quarries still operating today, Penrhyn is also one of the oldest and was the first to introduce terracing in 1799. This had two purposes: firstly it provided safer working conditions for the men and secondly the blocks of slate once dislodged did not have so far to fall and did not fragment into small, unusable blocks. At Penrhyn Quarry the terraces are on average 17 metres high and 12 metres wide. To loosen blocks of rock explosive charges are placed in holes drilled at right angles to the cleavage planes and carefully calculated to loosen, but not damage, the blocks of slate. In this way the rockmen are able to extract the largest size blocks manageable, which in turn will yield the largest and most expensive slates.

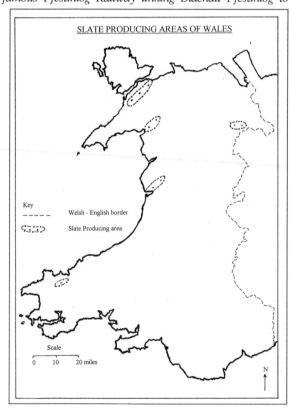

SLATE PRODUCING AREAS OF WALES

Key

- - - - Welsh - English border

⟨⊃⟩ Slate Producing area

Scale

0   10   20 miles

N

Blasting at Penrhyn Quarry, Bethesda, *c*. 1955. On each terrace can be seen the huts or *cabans* where the workmen ate their lunches. The plumes of smoke indicate where the charges have been detonated.

Quarrymen, Llechwedd, 1955. These two quarrymen working underground at Llechwedd are drilling holes to loosen the blocks of slates.

Transporting blocks of slate, 1964. Once the blocks have been loosened they are transported to the sheds where they can be reduced to a more manageable size. This tramway is at Bwlch Quarry, Llanberis.

Cutting blocks of slate, 1970. Once the blocks reach the sheds they are closely examined to determine where they should be cut. This is done with a diamond-tipped circular saw. The blocks are now ready for splitting.

Slate splitter, Penrhyn Quarry, 1962. Once blocks of slate have been extracted from the quarry they are carefully cut to make maximum use of each block. After cutting to a manageable size they are passed on to the slate splitter. Here at Penrhyn, John Emlyn Jones is using the traditional wooden mallet and bladed chisel, known in Welsh as *gordd hollti* and *cyn manhollt*, respectively. The block rests on his left leg while it is given a sharp tap along the cleavage plane causing it to split. It was usual for the splitter to protect his trousers from wear and tear by draping an old piece of cloth or carpet over his left leg. After splitting, the slates were then trimmed or 'dressed' to a number of standard sizes. In 1765 General Hugh Warburton, then owner of Penrhyn Quarry, decided on a number of standard sizes for his slates. These he called after female aristocratic titles. In ascending order of size they were ladies, viscountesses, countesses, marchionesses, small duchesses, duchesses, princesses and queens. This classification was widely adopted in North Wales and is still in use today. A 'lady' is 40 x 20cm in size, while a 'queen' is in excess of 75cm in length. The 'countess', at 25 x 50cm proved the most popular size. Despite attempts at mechanising the process of splitting slates, it is still the preserve of the skilled individual and likely to remain so.

Trimming slates, 1955. The final job is to trim the slates to the exact size required. Finished slates can be seen stacked in the background.

Teatime, Llechwedd, 1955. This is the interior of an underground *caban* in the Llechwedd slate mine. A whole culture grew up in each of these cabans which were renowned for the quality of their discussions on the political and social issues of the day.

Dinorwig Quarry, 1970. Like Penrhyn, Dinorwig Quarry is also terraced, but unlike its rival is on a hillside, not in a pit. The huts on the lakeside house the processing sheds where the slate blocks are cut down, split and the slates dressed before being shipped along the Padarn Railway to nearby Felinheli, once known as Port Dinorwic.

Velinheli and Dinorwic Slate Quarries, *c.* 1920. This postcard was produced by the then owners of the Dinorwig Quarry to publicise their products at a trade fair. The man sitting on the right is splitting slates, while his companion is dressing the slate to the correct size.

Y Felinheli, *c.* 1880. From Dinorwig, which in its heyday employed over 2,000 men, the slates were consigned via the Padarn Railway to Felinheli and hence to destinations across Europe and as far afield as Australia and the West Indies. The export of slates led to a thriving shipbuilding industry in many parts of North Wales.

Y Felinheli, *c.* 1880. A number of two-masted sailing vessels are waiting to load slates, including those visible in the foreground.

Blaenau Ffestiniog, Oakeley Quarries, 1901. The Oakeley Quarries grew through the amalgamation of eight smaller workings. In 1890 it was the third-largest slate quarry in Wales producing 60,000 tons of slate a year and employing 1,700 men. The workings extended from sea-level to 500 metres above sea-level and were arranged on 32 floors. There were reputed to be fifty miles of railway track underground as well as extensive tramways, some visible above, on the surface. The site had twelve dressing mills which together contained 53 dressing machines and 53 saw tables for trimming blocks of slate. Much use was made of steam power. There were also thirty workers' cottages and a hospital on the site.

The viaduct in the centre of the view gave access over the main-line Ffestiniog Railway. For every ton of slate extracted it was necessary to remove between nine and twelve tons of waste material. At some quarries this 'make to waste' ratio was far higher. At Aberllefenni near Corris the ratio at one time stood at 1:67. This quarry is still in operation but due to the use of modern rock-cutting methods the ratio is now 1:3.

Blaenau Festiniog, Oakeley Quarries, Top of C Incline. These three workmen are attending the two trams that have just ascended the incline. The shaley material on the top of the trams suggests that they contain waste material.

Blaenau Festiniog, Oakeley Quarries, Slate Splitters, 1901. Slate splitters from one of the dressing mills with examples of their work in the foreground.

Slates awaiting shipment, 1959. The finished product awaits shipment to Porthmadog along the Festiniog Railway and hence to destinations world-wide.

Quarrymen leaving work, Blaenau Ffestiniog, *c*. 1905. These quarrymen are leaving work on a device called a *car gwyllt* or velocipede. The devices were used exclusively at Craig Ddu Quarry, Blaenau Ffestiniog, until its closure in 1946.

Velocipede, Graig Ddu, 1959. Mr John Vaughan Davies, a retired quarryman, demonstrates his *car gwyllt* or velocipede which he originally bought for a guinea. When riding it he recalled that it was best to have a known competent rider both in front and behind you. As might be expected accidents happened and bones were sometimes broken. Velocipedes were invented by a local chemist and manufactured by Jonathan Ellis, blacksmith at Craig Ddu. They were made from a stout piece of wood such as a piece of railway sleeper, with a small wheel controlled by a brake clasped between the knees of the rider. A primitive Y-bracket at the back rested on the rail. A cranked iron strut spanned the gap between the two inner rails to provide balance. The device was light to carry and well-liked by the quarrymen as it turned the half-hour morning journey up the incline into a two-minute return journey at the end of the afternoon.

Craig Ddu Quarry was never a large concern and employed at most 110 men. It has the distinction of being the highest slate quarry in Wales being 600 metres above sea-level. Unlike other quarries in the Blaenau Ffestiniog area it has no underground workings.

Three

Coal

The coal measure rocks of South Wales were laid down in the Upper Carboniferous era approximately 300 million years ago. The conditions in which these rocks were first forried were those of tropical freshwater swamps dominated by tall trees, reeds and ferns. Organic matter such as leaves, branches and trunks accumulated to form thick layers of peat. The land mass on which they were accumulated was slowly subsiding subjecting the layers of peat to sporadic marine incursions covering the peat with layers of shale, sandstones and grit. These were followed by fine grained muds in which vegetation could flourish enabling the cycle to be repeated. As the peat is compacted by the weight of the sediments above water and gases are driven off and the peat is gradually converted to coal. Coal forms only 2 per cent of the South Wales coal measures, which are up to 2,400m thick in places.

Despite the relatively small size of the South Wales coalfield there is considerable variation in the type and quality of coal found. The reasons for this are not fully understood. In the eastern part of the coalfield the coal found is bituminous, i.e. it has a relatively high ash content, is quite soft, and best suited to use as house coal or converting to coke. In the Pembrokeshire coalfield the coal is anthracitic. Anthracite is a hard coal which has been subjected to much more intense heat and pressure than bituminous coal. Consequently it has a higher carbon content and burns with a very high heat leaving very little ash. Steam coal in South Wales is somewhere between the two, both geographically and in respect of its characteristics.

The earliest reference to the use of coal in Wales is at Neath in 1248. By 1750 coal was being used in both the copper industry centred around Swansea and the smelting of iron ore in other locations such as Merthyr Tudful and Blaenafon. As the century progressed, increasing quantities of sale-coal were being exported and coal production increased. Much of the labour at this time came from women and children, a situation that persisted until 1842 when a horrified Parliament heard evidence about working conditions and practices underground where children as young as seven were being employed.

By 1845 a number of developments such as the building of the Taff Vale Railway and the West Bute Dock in Cardiff combined to increase the amount of coal that could be exported outside the South Wales area, by now producing some 4.5 million tons per year. Of this figure 2 million tons were used by the iron industry, one million by the copper industry with the remainder ending up as sale-coal. The effect of these developments was dramatic; for example, in the parish of Aberdare 177,000 tons of coal were raised in 1844, but ten years later the figure was 1,009,000 tons.

In addition, many of the ironmasters also decided to enter the sale-coal business. Previously the ironmasters had only raised enough coal to supply their own ironworks, but now they saw a profitable opportunity for diversification. This had many advantages, for example, they could sell off coal found in their pits that was not suitable for use in blast furnaces. By increasing production they ensured there was always sufficient coal for the works despite labour unrest amongst the colliers who would restrict production in order to try and negotiate better pay and conditions. When only enough coal for daily use was being mined this was an effective tactic, but if sale-coal was also being raised then this could be diverted to the iron works, eliminating the workers' bargaining tool. Originally, leases were granted to the ironworks for the mineral rights and only a rental was paid, it being assumed that only sufficient coal for use in the ironworks would be mined. The increased activity generated by the sale-coal business led to friction between ironmasters and landowners who saw substantial profits being made which they were powerless to cash in on. Pits sunk by the ironmasters include Fochriw, near Dowlais, and Castle pit near Cyfarthfa. As the century progressed many pits sunk by the ironmasters became far more profitable than the ironworks, which subsequently closed. Examples of pits in this category include the Bryn-du and Cefn collieries near Bridgend.

Meanwhile, elsewhere, improvements in technology were leading to the introduction of more and more steamships. Much of the coal produced in the South Wales coalfield was ideally suited to use in steamships as it burnt with a good heat but gave out little smoke. When the Royal Navy gave South Wales coal their approval in 1851 it marked a phase of rapid expansion in the coalfield, especially in the Rhondda Valley where the population jumped from under 2,000 in 1851 to 152,000 in 1911.

The demand for steam coal, usually found at greater depths than bituminous coals, led to bigger and deeper pits being sunk, which in turn demanded greater capital expenditure. Thus limited liability companies were formed to exploit new resources and subsequently to purchase adjoining collieries. Amongst these were Powell Duffryn (known to their workforce as Poverty & Death) who by 1935 owned 75 collieries.

Instrumental in the development of the Rhondda was David Davies of Llandinam. He became a self-made millionaire, having starting out as a sawyer and building contractor in his native Montgomeryshire before winning a number of contracts to build railways in mid-Wales during the 1850s. By 1864 he had made a vast fortune and was looking for a new challenge. Steam coal was thought to underlie the Rhondda Valley but the depth at which it was likely to be found was the subject of much speculation and conjecture. With others, he took a lease of land from Crawshay Bailey and proceeded to sink a pit. Legend states that after many months of sinking the shaft the coal was nowhere to be seen. As he had spent £38,000 he decided that the work would have to stop and accordingly announced his decision to the workmen. After discussion amongst themselves the men agreed to give him a week's free labour and duly struck coal at a depth of 210 metres. By 1866 he had two collieries in production at Maindy and Park. He gave their product the title of Merthyr Ocean Coal to emphasise its suitability for steamships. He duly added further collieries to his portfolio and amassed another fortune along with the nickname 'Davies the Ocean'. In 1935 Ocean Coal Company owned 17 collieries.

The Universal Colliery at Senghenydd was developed in the 1890s by the Lewis Merthyr Company. It started to produce coal in 1895. By 1900 a thriving community of 5,000 adults and 900 children had developed, served by eight churches and chapels and various sporting and social clubs. The Universal pit had a reputation for being gassy and was to experience its first taste of disaster in 1901 when an explosion killed 82 men. This was to be eclipsed, however, on 14 October 1913 when an explosion in the west side of the mine, about two and a half miles from the shaft, killed a total of 439 men. The explosion occurred at about eight o'clock in the morning, two hours after the morning shift had started work. The eastern side of the mine was not affected and the five hundred or so men in that district were safely evacuated. Rescue parties sent down found a few survivors, including eighteen men at one location. Fires raging underground prevented a thorough search of the workings for more survivors. Evidence from the corpses brought to the surface suggested that most had been gassed by carbon monoxide rather than burnt. To alleviate the suffering relief funds were established by the Lord Mayors of London and Cardiff. Payments were made to the bereaved and the eight hundred miners rendered unemployed by the disaster.

On hearing of the disaster at Senghenydd a Glasgow photographer named Benton rushed to the village. He specialised in producing postcards of disasters and had produced cards of other such events. While this practice may seem odd by today's standards it must be remembered that newspapers then contained very few photographs and television was not available. Consequently, the public thirst for pictures of news stories was met to a large extent by postcards. It should also be noted that during the weekend following the disaster an estimated 100,000 sightseers descended on the village. Thus Benton's series of twenty-four cards of the disaster are fine examples of early-twentieth-century photojournalism. The pit was re-opened in late November of the same year, but eventually closed for good in 1928.

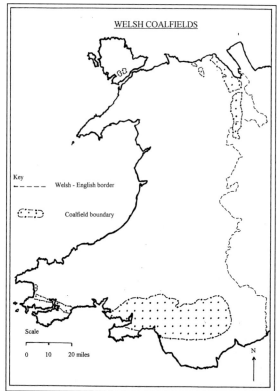

Accidents and fatalities were accepted as part and parcel of life by South Wales mining communities. While it was the large explosions that made newspaper headlines, these were not the major cause of death underground. During the period 1874-1914 a total of 2,578 miners were killed in explosions in the South Wales coalfield, but another 4,692 were killed by roof-falls. These tended to kill one or two miners at a time so rarely made the news. Another notable cause of death were accidents involving the cage. Underground hauliers also had exceptionally high rates of death and injury.

The peak year for coal production in Wales was 1913 when the South Wales coalfield produced 57 million tons and North Wales a further 3.5 million. This coal came from a total of 620 collieries employing the efforts of 232,800 men. During the First World War all collieries were temporarily nationalised in an effort to maximise production and afterwards returned to their owners.

After the Second World War the National Coal Board (NCB) was formed and on 1 January 1947 all collieries became the property of the state with the coal-owners being handsomely compensated for the loss of their pits. With nationalisation came the removal of piecework, i.e. payment depending on the amount of coal produced. Miners often cited this as a cause of accidents as it encouraged them to cut corners on safety. Instead the miners were now paid a fixed wage.

During the 1960s over 70 pits were closed as a result of rationalisation. All were deemed to be uneconomic to run. For some there was no market for the coal, in some reserves had been exhausted and in others difficult geological conditions precipitated their closure. Of those that remained much was invested in new technology rendering the pick and shovel methods inherited in 1947 obsolete. By 1975 there were 42 pits in operation in the South Wales coalfield and two in North Wales. In addition, output in Britain as a whole had risen to 2.5 tons of coal per miner per shift, up from one ton per miner per shift when the industry was nationalised. A further round of pit closures followed the year-long miners' strike in 1984-85 reducing the number of pits operating to 14, half the pre-strike level. In this period the workforce was also halved to 10,200 in South Wales.

31

Miners at Tower Colliery, *c.* 1991 (photograph by kind permission of Ron Davies). Today's colliers are far better equipped than their predecessors earlier this century who had little more than picks and shovels to hew out the coal.

Deep Navigation Colliery, Treharris, *c.* 1905. Deep Navigation was always one of the most profitable mines in Wales. Work on sinking the 750-metre shafts started in 1872 and took six years. At the time, they were the deepest in South Wales, being nearly 200 metres deeper than their rivals. Ocean Collieries bought the pit in 1883 and in 1915 the pit was the first in Wales to have pit-head baths installed. Most noticeable in this picture are the two head frames, one above each shaft. That on the right was powered from the engine house dominating the scene.

Oakwood Colliery, Maesteg, *c.* 1912. It was sunk in 1868. By the time this postcard was produced, shipping line Elder Dempster & Co. were the owners. Ovens were built nearby to convert the coal into coke for use in their vessels, most of which traded with West Africa. The company exported 250,000 tons of coal annually to Las Palmas where they supplied coal to the Admiralty and over 200 other shipping lines.

Pantyffynnon Colliery, *c.* 1925. Pantyffynnon Colliery near Ammanford, Carmarthenshire was an anthracite drift mine. The colliery survived nationalisation and in 1961 was employing 601 men. This general view shows the sheds over the coal screens, railway sidings and coal wagons. Unlike the views of Oakwood and Deep Navigation collieries there is no tower for the pit-head winding gear. Pits on the western side of the South Wales coalfield have easier access to coal reserves which are found nearer the surface. Entry to the mine is therefore by horizontal or inclined adits and the sinking of expensive shafts is not required. The photograph is one from a series by the Llandeilo-based photographer D.C. Harries dating from *c.* 1925.

Miners, Pantyffynnon, *c*. 1925. The miners are ascending on coal trams after their shift. Note the safety lamps and tins being carried.

Winding gear, Pantyffynnon, *c*. 1925. Winding at Pantyffynnon Colliery was achieved by a single-action, high-pressure steam engine, which in contrast to the rest of the mine seems to have been kept spotlessly clean.

Point of Ayr Colliery, Ffynnongroyw, *c.* 1920. The North Wales coalfield at one time comprised some forty pits and employed 15,000 people in the counties of Denbighshire and Flintshire. Until 1875 there was also one mine in Anglesey producing low-quality coal. The coalfield extends under the River Dee in the north and to the east into England. The best-known pits in the coalfield were Gresford, Bersham and Point of Ayr. The peak year for production was 1929 when 3.5 million tons were raised. Gresford is remembered for the colliery explosion in 1934 when 265 miners perished in the worst mining disaster since Senghenydd. By the 1950s only eight pits remained, but produced some two million tons per year. The closure of Gresford in 1972 and Bersham in 1986 now leaves Point of Ayr as the sole surviving deep mine in the coalfield.

Situated on the banks of the River Dee, Point of Ayr Colliery marks the most northerly tip of Wales. The two shafts go down to a depth of over 200 metres, the workings extending out under the sea. A consequence of the coastal location of the colliery was the ability for ships to load with coal directly from the wharf on the right of the mine. Prior to nationalisation the colliery ran its own fleet of steamers to deliver coal. Ships continued to use this facility up until 1948. By 1953 Point of Ayr Colliery employed 738 men and produced 213,000 tons of coal. Production at the mine commenced in 1890 and continues to the present day.

Winding men up, Pandy Pit, Tonypandy.

Winding men up, Pandy Pit, Tonypandy, *c.* 1930. For every miner the working day began with the journey down the shaft in the cage. After reaching the pit-bottom the journey continued until the workings were reached. In some of the older pits this could entail a journey of up to three miles from the shaft. These miners with their coal-blackened faces have just completed their shift. The next shift is waiting to go down. Notice that the men in the cage are standing on rails for the trams. Between the rails is a device to hold the trams in place. Note that the cage can accommodate two trams on different levels.

Within each pit there was a hierarchy amongst the miners based largely on the job done and wages received. At the top were the colliers, those engaged in hewing the coal at the coal face. These were followed by the repairers, frequently older men, who were responsible for keeping the roadways in good order, replacing defective timbers and props and tidying up after any roof falls. Lower down the hierarchy were the hauliers responsible for moving the trams between the stalls and the cage. This was a dangerous job as hauliers were frequently crushed and liable to be kicked by the pit ponies that pulled the trams. Apart from the boys in the mine the lowest paid were labourers and ostlers.

On the surface were more occupations, some such as smiths and farriers, well-paid and skilled men. The majority were labourers, often older men no longer able to work underground. Their jobs included dressing coal and loading railway wagons and although also classed as labourers they received lower wages than their counterparts underground.

Coal mining, colliers at work, *c*. 1905. This is one of a series of postcards produced by Stephen Timothy, a photographer from Ton Pentre, Rhondda. All were taken underground in the Tonpentre level. Two colliers are working at the coal face while a third is engaged in timbering, i.e. putting pit props in place to hold the roof up after the coal has been hewn out. Between the two colliers at the coal face is the curling box used for loading lumps of coal into the trams. The job of filling the trams was the responsibility of the colliers. Usually it would be left to the collier's boy or apprentice. He had to be sure to fill the trolley with lumps of coal as any fragments or coal dust would be discarded when the tram was weighed. Apprentices worked under the supervision of other colliers for five years before being given their own stall to work. Usually they would serve their apprenticeships under older relatives, often brothers. Before being taken away each tram would be chalked to identify which collier had filled it. Colliers, pre-nationalisation, were paid on the basis of how much coal they sent to the surface.

Coal mining, *c.* 1905. Geological conditions in the South Wales coalfield often conspired against the collier. Many seams were less than a metre thick and forced the collier to crouch or lie down as he worked, often in water. The colliers are using their picks to chip away at the base of the coal seam, thus weakening the coal with the aim of extracting the coal in large lumps.

Haulier bringing the coal out, c. 1905. This pit pony is hauling a truck of coal from the coal-face to the base of the shaft. In 1913 there were over 17,000 horses working underground in South Wales.

Putting coal into the carriage at pit-bottom, c. 1905. The tram has reached the bottom of the shaft and is waiting to be hauled to the top in the cage.

Weighing the coal, *c.* 1925. Once the trams had reached the surface a note was made of the chalk marks on the side and the tram and contents weighed. This was done by two men, a weigher and a check-weigher. The latter was a representative of the miners there to see that the correct weight was recorded. The tram in this view is on the weighbridge while the weigher writes down the weight.

Tipping coal, *c.* 1925. After weighing, the coal was tipped out of the trams, usually with a rotary tippler, such as this one at Pantyffynnon Colliery. The tram is held firmly in place and inverted to tip the coal through screens which sort the coal by size, then on to conveyor belts for dressing and washing.

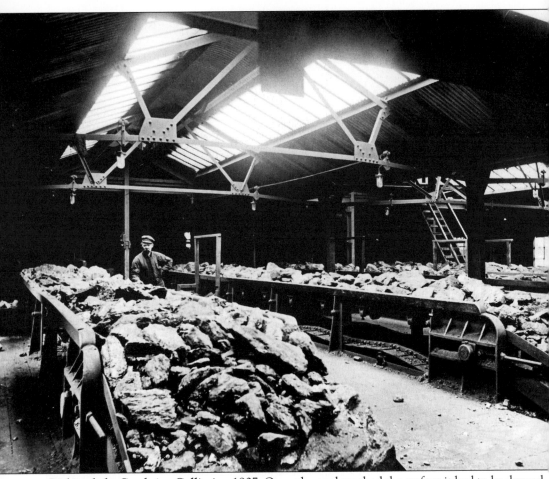

Picking belt, Cambrian Collieries, 1907. Once the coal reached the surface it had to be dressed and sorted by size. Dressing the coal was often done by boys too young to go underground, women, or older, sometimes, disabled workers no longer fit to work underground. The process involved checking that no waste material such as rock or timber was to be found amongst the lumps of coal.

Small coal and coal dust (culm) were often used to make bricks of patent fuel by crushing the coal into a powder, mixing with bitumen and shaping into bricks.

Pay-day at Glamorgan Collieries, Llwynypia, *c.* 1910. The miners milling around in the colliery yard are waiting to be rewarded for their hours of toil. The face workers are distinguishable from the surface workers by their blackened faces. When this postcard was published *c.* 1910, pit-head baths were still a thing of the future. Instead, bathing was done at home in a tin tub.

A train leaving the collieries for Barry Docks, 1907. The Welsh coalfield is fortunate that no pit is more than thirty miles from the sea making export far easier and cheaper than many other coalfields. Most South Wales coal was destined for the boilers of steamships.

Coal in the process of shipment at Barry Dock, 1907. On arrival at the docks the wagons would discharge their load through coal tips or hoists into ships waiting below. These wagons from Cambrian Collieries are discharging their coal directly into the hold of the 1,278-ton steamer Collingwood, owned by Furness, Withy & Co. of West Hartlepool.

Cwm Colliery rescue team, *c.* 1910. Every colliery had at least one rescue team of trained men ready to assist at their own or a nearby colliery and familiar with all aspects and dangers of coal mining. Note the hooded masks and oxygen bags around their chests. Rescue teams would often take a caged canary with them to give an early warning of gas.

The Universal Pit, Senghenydd, where over 400 miners were entombed on Tuesday, Oct. 14th 1913.

The Universal pit, Senghenydd, where over 400 miners were entombed on Tuesday, 14 October 1913. The overall layout of the pit can be seen – the headgear, chimneys and railway sidings all clearly visible. The final death toll was 439.

Welsh Pit Disaster. The scene at the Pithead hour by hour all through the Day. Benton 138 George ST Glasgow. 20.

Welsh pit disaster – the scene at the pithead hour by hour all through the day. The disaster left behind 250 widows and 542 fatherless children. One woman lost her husband, three sons and four brothers, whilst in one row of eleven houses no less than twenty men perished.

Welsh Pit Disaster. Local Clergy giving help. Benton 138 George ST Glasgow. 15.

Welsh pit disaster – local clergy giving help. A clergyman attempts to console a grieving widow.

Welsh pit disaster. A street in Senghenydd. A victim in every house.

Welsh pit disaster. A street in Senghenydd. A victim in every house. Known as 'the huts', these one-storey dwellings with one window, a front door and chimney stack were built quickly and cheaply *c.* 1893 to accommodate the 'sinkers' – those men responsible for sinking the shafts. They later housed miners and their families.

The Great Welsh disaster at Senghenydd. Removing some of the Victims.

The Great Welsh disaster at Senghenydd. Removing some of the victims. Most of the men died as a result of carbon monoxide poisoning following the explosion.

Miners protesting against closure, Tower Colliery, 1993. (By kind permission of Aled Jenkins). Tower Colliery near Hirwaun was originally threatened with closure despite making £23 million for British Coal in the two years preceding the threat of closure. Instead of allowing the pit to close, the workforce banded together behind an employee-buy-out scheme. Each of the 239 miners invested £8,000 of redundancy money to enable them to buy the pit, now the last remaining deep mine in the South Wales valleys. Tower was in profit after only three months and produced a pre-tax profit of £3.6 million in its first full year after the buy-out.

Four

Fishing

In Wales, as elsewhere, fishing is as old as civilisation itself and takes many forms. Methods such as cockle gathering have remained almost unchanged over centuries, while the coracle dates back to prehistoric times.

For Wales as a whole herring was the most widespread and important catch, the fish being particularly abundant in Cardigan Bay and along the North Wales coast. Herring fishing took place usually between August and February with the fishermen often otherwise employed as farmers or tradesmen. The fish were preserved by smoking or pickling in brine or a combination of both. Herring formed an important export for many small rural communities as well as providing cheap and nourishing food for the local inhabitants. Villages such as Aberporth and Nefyn were famed for their herring, but like the other ports once famous for their herring the industry was in decline at the start of this century and had died out in most places by 1939. The only exceptions were Cardiff, Swansea and Milford Haven, the latter now being the only port landing herring in significant quantities.

Milford Haven came to prominence as a port in the last quarter of the nineteenth century. Docks had been built with the hope of attracting transatlantic trade and rivalling Bristol and Liverpool as a major port. The sought-after trade did not arrive, however, and the town was forced to settle for the less glamorous role of fishing port, complete with quayside market, ice-making factories and, by 1914, 63 steam trawlers. Employment, directly and indirectly from the fishing industry was estimated at two thousand. By the 1920s the town was the largest fishing port in Wales and fourth largest in Britain. There is now, however, little fishing activity at Milford Haven and what remains is linked to the activities of Spanish-owned vessels rather than locally owned trawlers.

At the start of this century there were 150 cockle gatherers at Ferryside and over 500 in the Carmarthen Bay area. Until the 1950s Carmarthen Bay accounted for a third of all cockles harvested in Britain. The gatherers, exclusively women until the 1960s, would gather cockles on Monday, Tuesday and sometimes Wednesday. Thursday was reserved for boiling and shelling cockles either outdoors or in small communal factories. Today all cockles are prepared in factories, most of which are little more than huts. Friday and Saturday were devoted to selling the cockles in markets such as Swansea and Carmarthen or door-to-door in the South Wales valleys.

To gather the cockles, which are found in beds 20cm below the surface of the sand, a small knife and a hand-rake are used. They are then sieved to remove any that are undersized and placed in sacks. Sieves can be seen balanced on the back of the donkeys. (See overleaf).

Welsh cockle gatherers, Ferryside, *c.* 1905. This method of gathering cockles has changed little in over a hundred years. Until the 1960s donkeys, which could carry only 3 cwt, were used to transport cockles from the beach. The replacement of the donkey with horse-drawn rubber-tyred carts in the 1970s and the consequent over-harvesting was one reason suggested for the decline in cockle numbers.

Cockle women preparing for boiling, Penclawdd, *c.* 1950. The cocklewomen with their sacks are waiting their turn to boil the cockles and remove them from the shells. After boiling and washing they are kept in baskets ready to take to market. Note the vast numbers of cockle shells underfoot.

A misty morning on the Conwy, *c.* 1900. The Conwy estuary is famous for mussels, once prized for pearls but now harvested from September to April for consumption. Mussels are collected by hand at low-water or from small open boats using a long-handled rake to scrape the mussels from the sea-bed. Here the mussel gatherers have been at work, evidenced by a sack on the left. Protruding from the boat on the right is the handle of a long rake. Dredging is in progress in the background.

Coracle fishermen on the Teifi at Cenarth, *c.* 1920. Note the net drying on the right.

Salmon fishing in the Dyfi, Glandyfi, Cardiganshire, *c.* 1920. In the rivers and estuaries of Wales salmon fishing is widely practised, and on rivers such as the Tywi and Teifi coracles are still used. Coracles can be traced back to prehistoric times. They are made of canvas or flannel dipped in tar and tacked onto a willow frame. Each coracle weighs about 15 kg and will last for about two years.

Fishing from coracles is usually done with a net spread between two coracles. Legal stipulations state that nets currently in use on the Teifi for this method of fishing are no more than 6 metres long and 1.2 metres deep. Coracles fish in pairs, starting four or five metres apart. The net is drawn in gradually by the coracle on the left-hand side until the coracles are touching.

Salmon fishing on the Dyfi is conducted in a slightly different fashion. One fisherman stands on the shore holding one end of the net. Two others go out in a boat, as shown above, one to row and the other to pay out the net. The boat is rowed in a semi-circle back to the shore whilst the net, usually about 100 metres but sometimes 200 metres long is paid out. On reaching the shore the boat is secured and the net hauled in. The top of the net has cork floats attached to it, visible in the photograph, whilst the bottom of the net is weighted with lead or stones. This arrangement keeps the net vertical in the water. Called seine-netting, this method of fishing is the most common form of commercial fishing on the river estuaries of Wales.

The Docks, Milford Haven, *c.* 1935. By far the most important part of the fishing industry in economic terms were the fleets of trawlers that once operated out of ports such as Tenby, Cardiff and Milford Haven. The trawlers at Milford Haven, keenly watched by gulls looking for scraps, were once part of a fleet that in 1925 totalled 110 vessels.

Entrance to the Docks, Milford Haven, *c.* 1912. Coal wagons can be seen on the quayside. Each trawler would burn up to eight tons of coal a day. While at sea the catch was kept fresh using ice from one of the ice-making factories on the dock side. Two chimneys from such factories can also be seen.

The Fish Wharf, Swansea, *c*. 1900. Fish was processed in quayside factories or sold in the local fish market, as at Swansea. Local fish sellers would then take them around surrounding areas, first by hand-cart, later by motor-van. At smaller ports, such as Aberystwyth, no market existed and fish sellers would negotiate with the fishermen on the quayside. They would then take their hand-carts through the town to favoured pitches to sell their wares.

Fresh mackerel, *c*. 1925. Mrs Thomas with her hand-cart selling mackerel on the promenade at Aberystwyth.

Tenby Harbour, *c.* 1890. Tenby, known in Welsh as Dinbych-y-pysgod (Tenby of the fish) was an important fishing port for centuries until the construction of the harbour at Milford Haven lured many boats away with the offer of better facilities. The view below, dating from *c.* 1890, shows the harbour almost overflowing with one and two-masted sailing vessels. The two-masted vessel on the right is drying her sails.

Tenby Harbour, 1927, showing remnants of the town's fishing fleet. These are mainly single-masted sailing vessels that fished with nets or, more rarely, long lines of baited hooks. Some Tenby boats also engaged in dredging for oysters. Even at this time most fishermen would have spent the summer months taking visitors on trips around the bay.

Tenby Harbour, *c.* 1960. The harbour is now dominated by pleasure craft, mainly yachts and cabin cruisers. Only a few fishing boats can be seen, moored nearest the sea to enable them to enter and leave with the minimum of inconvenience. This is a scene repeated throughout the coastal towns and villages of Wales.

At Freshwater West, *c.* 1930. The harvest of the sea is not confined just to fish. The rush-roofed huts on the beach at Freshwater West were used to store and dry a species of seaweed called Porphyra. This is better known by the name 'laverbread' and is a popular local delicacy.

New Quay, *c.* 1965. These fishermen are repairing lobster pots. New Quay, three miles south of Aberaeron, Ceredigion is one of a number of small villages on the shores of Cardigan Bay that once relied heavily on herring. Since 1945 lobster fishing has become increasingly significant. Lobster pots are made of willow, plastic or, as here, wire, to which fishermen fix netting and a blob of concrete at the base to weigh it down.

Net mending, New Quay, *c.* 1970 (photograph by kind permission of Ron Davies). Local fisherman Winston Evans is seen here repairing his herring nets ready for the forthcoming season.

Llewellyn Hookes, Abersoch, fisherman, 1961. Such is the level of lobster fishing in Cardigan Bay that each lobster will be caught numerous times before it is large enough to be taken. The cage on the left is for holding the caught lobsters.

Five

Lead Mining

The history of lead mining in Wales can be traced back to Roman times. The industry reached its peak during the middle of the last century when lead was mined in every county in Wales except for Anglesey. The counties most noted for lead mining were Flintshire, Cardiganshire and Glamorganshire. Today most counties are scarred by barren waste tips and ruined buildings marking the site of these endeavours. Attempts are being made in many places to landscape the sites and alleviate the problems, especially water pollution associated with the workings.

Lead ore is usually found in the form of galena, chemical formula PbS. Frequently lead is found in conjunction with other metaliferous ores such as silver, zinc and copper as well as worthless 'gangue' minerals such as quartz and calcite. The lead ore is found in veins which have been injected as fluids into the Silurian country rock at high temperature and great depth and pressure. This hydrothermal mineralisation took place over periods of many millions of years during the Carboniferous era. Subsequent tectonic movement has raised these rocks to the surface and the reach of man.

There were two methods of extracting the ore. Where it outcropped near the surface the overburden would be removed to reveal the veins (also called lodes) of ore. This method, similar to quarrying, is called open-cast mining. Usually, however, the lead was found deep underground. To reach it a series of interconnecting vertical shafts and horizontal adits had to be dug. These would follow the course of the veins.

During the last century lead was much in demand to make water piping, roofing, paint and munitions. The reasons for the decline of the lead industry are complex but were related to the relatively high price of British ore compared with competitors such as Spain and, after 1880, Australia. Another factor that led to the decline of lead mining in Wales were the activities of unscrupulous entrepreneurs who raised money for mining concerns purely with the aim of making a large profit. In some instances working capital was used to pay huge dividends, thus driving up the price of the shares which the directors would promptly sell leaving shareholders with a worthless company. Another ruse was to spend lavishly on dressing mills and other above ground facilities to infer prosperity, float the company on the stock market and sell their holdings at a tidy profit, again leaving shareholders with a worthless company. As such ruses became more and more commonplace efforts to raise funds by legitimate mining concerns were thwarted. Today, lead is no longer mined in Wales, the last mine closing in 1958.

Cwmystwyth Lead Mines, Cardiganshire, *c.* 1920. Cwmystwyth is situated fourteen miles to the east of Aberystwyth and was the largest lead mine in Cardiganshire. During the 1850s it was producing 1,200 tons of lead ore a year. In addition, silver was found in sufficiently high concentrations to make it worthwhile extracting. At the turn of the century the attention of the owners turned to the extraction of zinc ore. This had previously been regarded as a gangue (waste) mineral, but with the introduction of galvanisation became a sought-after metal.

Lead mining at Cwmystwyth goes back nearly a thousand years. For example, monks from nearby Strata Florida Abbey used lead that they themselves had mined. Both underground and open-cast mining were practised at Cwmystwyth. In the picture the scars left by open-cast mining can be seen above the mine buildings. In the centre of the photo is a row of houses called Neville Place built to house miners and their families. Unmarried miners were accommodated in the Barracks, the four-storey building to the right of Neville Place.

Cwmystwyth Mines, *c.* 1910. This second view of the mine buildings is dominated by the corrugated, iron-clad dressing mill. Lead ore was fed in at the top where it was crushed between two heavy rollers. The crushed ore was then placed in buddles (hoppers filled with water) which were agitated so that the lead ore fell to the bottom while the lighter waste material could be washed off. The ore concentrate was then dried and bagged ready for despatch to a smeltery. The small buildings below the mill house were where gas to power the other machinery was produced. Next to this can be seen piles of fine rock waste. The row of buildings on the right comprise the mine manager's offices, the assay laboratory, smithy and paymaster's office. On the extreme left facing the other buildings are the stables. On the right is an older crushing mill. Like most mines in mid-Wales power for crushing, pumping and hauling was provided by water-power as coal was not found locally and was too expensive to import.

Dylife' Lead Mines.

Dylife Lead Mines, c. 1910. Lead mining at Dylife, some ten miles from Machynlleth, is thought to go back to Roman times. However, it was during the middle of the last century that Dylife was most active. One of the most noteworthy features of Dylife was an attempt to mechanise the mine and bring it on a par with collieries. To this end a cage and trams were installed. Most lead mines at this time, and for many decades to come relied on a large bucket, called a kibble, on a rope for removing ore and an exhausting series of ladders to enable the miners to reach their workings. As though to repay the mine-owners for their far-sightedness, in 1862 the 250 miners employed raised a staggering 2,571 tons of lead ore, a figure only subsequently exceeded in mid-Wales by the Van mine near Llanidloes. Such prosperity did not last, however, and after 1870 the mine could not produce even half of this figure.

Despite various attempts at resuscitation the mine never regained its former glories. A resurgence in the price of lead in the 1920s saw a revival of interest but this was short-lived. The village of Dylife, which once boasted a community of nearly a thousand souls, followed the lead mine into dereliction and is today little more than a scattered community of small cottages.

Van Lead Mine, near Llanidloes, *c*. 1910. The large deposits of ore underlying Y Fan near Llanidloes were first discovered in the 1850s, but not adequately developed until the 1860s. When the Van Mining Company was floated on the stock market the £5 shares rose to £86 in a year. This led to a number of new mining concerns springing up, often incorporating the word Van in their titles. Van mines produced over 70,000 tons of lead ore and 25,000 tons of zinc blende up until 1884. Its greatest single year was 1876 when nearly 9,000 tons of ore were raised by the 700 employees. As already mentioned the decline in lead-ore prices due to foreign imports led to the closure of many mines and even the great Van was not immune.

Most lead mines, including Cwmystwyth, Dylife and Van, were to be found in relatively remote areas away from large settlements. As a consequence coal was expensive to import for use as a fuel. Instead, the miners used another great Welsh resource – water – to power the mines. Reservoirs were built and the water channelled along leats to work water-wheels at the mines. Water-wheels could pump water, power the crushing machinery and haul ore from the bottom of the shaft through a system of gears. In many instances water would be used to operate wheels at a whole series of mines aligned down a valley.

Bwlch-Glas Lead Mine, Talybont, 1907. In 1907 the price of lead ore increased markedly and reached £20 per ton. Some previously uneconomic mines now became viable. One such mine was Bwlch-glas, near Talybont in Dyfed. In 1907 a new company – 'Scottish Cardigan Mines Ltd' – was formed to re-open the mine. This was the first mine in Mid Wales to use a gas plant as the source of power. Until its closure in 1916 the mine produced 1,240 tons of ore. In the postcard the tramway from the workings can be seen on the extreme right. This led to the crushing plant (with the sloping roof) and hence to the ore concentration plant with the rounded roof.

Six
Wool

Although mid-Wales is the area most associated with the woollen industry, woollen mills were scattered across the whole of Wales. Most were established to serve the needs of the local community producing material for clothes, blankets, etc. The mills were usually run on a part-time basis, the owner often having a smallholding as well. Many of the transactions of these mills would have been by bartering – the farmer offering a portion of his wool, often half, in exchange for having the rest turned into cloth or goods. Alternatively, agricultural produce would be exchanged for making the wool into cloth. Often those employed in the mill would also be paid partly with goods. These rural mills employed perhaps ten or fifteen workers and were invariably sited next to a fast-flowing stream used both to wash the wool and power the machinery via a water-wheel. Woollen goods were exported from Wales on a larger scale from the start of the nineteenth century and at one time were popular for clothing slaves in the USA.

During the third quarter of the nineteenth century Newtown and Llanidloes developed as centres for the processing of wool and a number of factories were built bringing the entire production process under one roof for the first time. Their construction led to the decline of the small rural mills. The arrival of the railway in the early 1860s allowed both easier export of the finished goods and also the importation of coal to provide steam power. As the demand for wool for these factories could not be satisfied locally the factories used the services of wool merchants and fellmongers to obtain wool for them from other parts of Britain and abroad. Despite the arrival of the railway, by the 1880s the industry was in decline, mainly due to competition from larger, more modern mills in Lancashire and Yorkshire. These produced cheaper goods and were in direct competition with the Montgomeryshire mills.

One venture that bucked this trend was that of Pryce Jones of Newtown who in 1859 established one of the first mail-order businesses in Britain. Initially, he sold almost exclusively Welsh flannel products, some of which were made at his Severn Valley Mills, also in Newtown. By the mid-1860s he was able to claim Florence Nightingale and Queen Victoria as his customers. In 1879 he moved to the specially-built Royal Welsh Warehouse near the railway station, was employing 300 people and claimed to have 100,000 customers. However, by this time the products of the Welsh woollen industry were only responsible for a small portion of the company's turnover. At its peak the company claimed a quarter of a million customers, had its own post office and in 1887 earned a knighthood for its founder, Sir Pryce Pryce-Jones who served as Conservative MP for Montgomery Boroughs on two occasions.

Another area in which the industry became increasingly concentrated was in north Carmarthenshire and southern Cardiganshire, most notably around Llandysul, Pentre-cwrt and Dre-fach Felindre. Development took place from 1880 onwards when power looms were introduced and larger, integrated mills employing up to one hundred people built. Most of the products, especially flannel, shirts, underwear and shawls from these mills were sold in industrial South Wales. Many of these new mills had very up-to-date equipment and relied on anthracite coal from the western coalfield to provide power. Thus a location near a railway line became as important as the traditional location near a stream or river. The high point for the industry in this area came during the First World War when the mills were at full stretch making uniforms and blankets for the war effort. Almost inevitably the 1920s saw a decline in the industry due in part to the reluctance of many owners to invest in new plant, the sale of large quantities of army surplus material, a miners' strike in 1921 and the arrival of cheaper cotton substitutes. By 1922, of a total of 151 woollen mills in Wales, 92 were to be found in Cardiganshire and Carmarthenshire. This number had fallen to 49 out of 71 by 1947.

The processing of wool into cloth is one that involves a number of processes. The first is to sort the wool into different grades. The breed of sheep from which the fleece comes affects the quality of the wool, as does the part of the fleece from which the wool is taken. Once the wool has been sorted it had to be washed and scoured to remove impurities such as earth, dust and vegetable matter. Usually soda ash, soap and warm water were used. Following cleansing the wool would, if required, be dyed. Prior to the third quarter of the last century natural dyes made out of leaves, berries, bark and roots were used, but after 1856 artificial alternatives became available. Some smaller Welsh mills, however, continued to use natural dyes until the 1930s. Some mills preferred to dye the wool after it had been woven into lengths of cloth. After dying, the raw wool is willowed to disentangle the fibres and open it out ready for the next stage, known as carding. Vegetable oil is added to replace the natural oils removed during washing and scouring before carding commences. Usually favoured as the best time to blend different quality wools, carding involves breaking down the natural alignment of the wool fibres to form a ribbon-like uniform web from which slivers can be spun. It is an important process in that if the wool is not carded correctly the fault cannot be remedied later. After carding the woollen fibres still require twisting together to give them strength. Carding machines were used for the process from the early nineteenth century onwards.

Spinning imparts strength to the thread by twisting and compressing the fibres in the slivers so that each fibre is intertwined with its neighbour. It is then stretched, lengthening the thread and causing longitudinal compression. The final process involved in converting wool into cloth is weaving, whereby the threads are interlaced at right angles to each other. Originally this was done by hand-looms. More efficient and quicker power-looms, often obtained second-hand from mills in Yorkshire began to be introduced throughout Wales late in the nineteenth century.

Royal Welsh Warehouse and Factory, *c.* 1905. Pryce-Jones's Royal Welsh Warehouse is on the left and the factory, built in 1895, is on the right. The limit of the arched windows on the second floor of the warehouse reveals the extent of the original building opened in 1879. Two further phases of development followed, culminating in the building of the bridge linking the warehouse and the factory in 1901.

Spring Mills, Llanidloes, *c.* 1868. This was one of fifteen such factories to be found in Llanidloes at various times during the nineteenth century. Built in 1875, it closed in 1908 and was converted into a tannery. The small wheels in the foreground mark the track on which the spindle carriage travels.

Lerry Mill Wheel, Talybont, *c.* 1955. Founded in 1809, this mill employed 30 people in 1900. It was one of four mills in the village, and operated until the 1960s using hand-looms. Most mills were at one time operated by water-power, hence the water-wheel.

Cwm Factory, Talybont, 1898. The spinning machine or 'mule' works by drawing the slivers out from the bobbins on the right. After a length has been drawn the machine stops paying the slivers out whilst the spindle carriage on the left moves away from the bobbins stretching and tightening the yarn. On its return the carriage winds the yarn on to the sixty or so spindles.

Hand-looms, Talybont, *c.* 1905. Another view from Talybont shows weavers at work using hand-looms. A roll of finished cloth can be seen under the loom. Much of the produce from these mills was to supply the needs of local lead miners.

Bryncir Mill, *c*. 1960. Bryncir Mill near Garndolbenmaen was converted from a corn mill to a woollen mill in the 1830s. The mill supplied cloth and clothing to the slate quarrymen of the district and later in the markets at Tremadoc and Porthmadog where the seafaring community purchased many of the mill's goods. It was not until 1916, when the mill-owner purchased a motor-car, that goods from Brynkir were sold farther afield. Still operating today, the mill is a popular tourist attraction.

Above, two yarns are being combined to give a thicker and stronger thread in a process known as doubling. Stronger thread is required for some products such as bedspreads, at one time a speciality of the mill.

Weaving bedspreads, *c.* 1960. Two types of bedspreads are being woven on power-looms at Bryncir. The one on the left is of Tapestry design, that below Honeycomb.

Seven

Tinplate

The tinplate industry developed in South Wales as an offshoot of the iron and steel industries. Tinplate manufacture comprises of flattening steel bars to the required thickness and size and coating the plates with a layer of tin. The industry developed in the Llanelli/Swansea area due to the availability of the raw materials required – coal, water and iron. The tin itself came initially from nearby Cornwall. Unlike iron and steel works tinplate mills were not so capital-intensive and could be set up relatively cheaply encouraging entrepreneurs from other industries to invest. This led to a proliferation of tinplate mills in the area during the nineteenth century. Towns such as Morriston, Pontardawe and Pontardulais developed around the industry and South Wales was responsible for the entire British output of tinplate. Typical of these small mills was the Clayton Tinplate Company Limited which took over the ailing Pontardulais Tinplate Works in 1883. This works went on to produce milk-churns, railway-lamp reflectors and gas-meters. The photographs on the following pages were all taken at the Clayton works shortly before closure in 1957.

By 1891, out of a total of 525 tinplate mills in the United Kingdom, 502 were in South Wales. Being cheap, light, strong and easily soldered, tinplate was used for a variety of household products such as candlesticks, lanterns, buckets, funnels, jugs and food-handling utensils. The greatest market by far was for the canning of food. Most tinplate goods were exported, especially to North America where its uses included tins for meat and oildrums. In fact, in 1891, only a quarter of tinplate produced in Britain was for the home market. The industry suffered a sharp decline shortly after 1891 due to imposition of a tariff by the US government on imported tinplate. This led to liquidation of some firms and emigration to the United States by many skilled workers. However, new markets were found in Europe and the British Empire and the industry recovered. By the 1930s further erosion of market share took place as numerous countries including Italy, Belgium, India, Canada and Norway started manufacturing tinplate. This was a double blow as these countries ceased importing Welsh tinplate and also started to compete in other export markets.

A notable first for the tinplate industry in Llanelli at this time was achieved in 1935 when the Felinfoel Brewery started selling beer in tins. This was the first tinned beer in Europe and followed closely on developments in the United States. It was no coincidence that this event took place in Llanelli as the John family, owners of the brewery, also had interests in the St Davids Tinplate Works at Bynea.

The pattern of numerous plants operating small hand-mills that developed in the nineteenth century was to remain in place until after the Second World War when the availability of new technology led to the polarisation of the industry at new large plants, a process that had started with the opening of a tinning line at the new Ebbw Vale steelworks in 1938, later converting the tinning process from baths of molten tin to an electrolytic tinning line. Restructuring of the industry came about with government assistance through the Tinplate Redundancy Scheme. Remaining tinplate producers were encouraged to amalgamate with steel producers to form the Steel Company of Wales and were thus able to build new and up-to-date mills. Their first project was the building of the giant strip mill at Port Talbot to supply new tinplate works opened at Trostre (1953) and Felindre (1956).

These new mills used long coils rather than individual sheets of steel for much of the process and were able to work far more efficiently than the old mills. At Ebbw Vale gases from the blast furnaces and the coke ovens could be used in the annealing process, thus cutting down on energy costs. These new plants rely on electrolysis rather than dipping the sheets into molten tin. Electrolysis involves transferring metal, in this case tin, from one electrode (anode) to the other (cathode) by passing an electric current through the solution in which both are immersed. Electrolytic tinning is a continuous process that encompasses electrolytic cleaning and pickling, electro-deposition of the tin by using a bar of tin as the anode whilst the steel strip acts as the cathode. Both are immersed in a bath of phenosulphonic acid. The plated strip then undergoes flow melting (heating the tin very rapidly to get a mirror like finish), and finally oiling to protect the surface.

Along with the tinplate operations at Richard Thomas & Baldwin's Ebbw Vale works, the Steel Company of Wales works were re-nationalised in 1967 as part of British Steel. Now privatised, they are still part of British Steel plc.

General view of the bar bank, 1957. The first process in the making of tinplate is receiving the steel sheet. This is unloaded from the railway wagons by overhead cranes and placed in the storing bank. For safety reasons sheets at the Clayton Works were never stored in piles above five feet high.

Cutting bars to length, 1957. The next stage is to cut the bars to the appropriate size before they are heated then rolled.

Rollerman entering a 'piece of singles' into roller, 1957. After heating, the bars are passed through the roughing rolls. Behind the rolls is the catcher whose job is to pass the bar back over the top of the rolls for the process to be repeated. Once the bar is twice the size of the sheets required it is folded over and again passed through the rollers. Eventually eight sheets of steel, now known as rough blackplate, will have been extracted from the one original bar.

Opening plates, 1957. Once sheets of rough blackplate have been rolled it is important to separate them to prevent them sticking together and allow slight oxidation. This was traditionally done by women known as 'openers'. Due to the sharp edges on the plates it was important that protective clothing – canvas apron, gloves and gauntlet – was worn.

Black pickling department, 1957. To remove the traces of oxidation the plates are dipped in batches into a vat of either sulphuric or hydrochloric acid and then rinsed in clean water. This is known as black pickling. The rack containing the plates is about to be immersed in acid.

Placing cover over packed plates ready for annealing, 1957. The next stage is to soften the plates by heating them gently for up to ten hours and allowing them to cool naturally. This is called annealing and makes the plates easier to stamp into shape subsequently. Sand is placed at the bottom of the box to keep it airtight.

A dipper lowering a plate into pure tin, 1957. After white pickling the plate is ready to be immersed in molten tin. This was a labour-intensive and skilful job, relying on the dexterity of the workman to give the plate an even coat of tin.

Cleaning heavy-coated tinplate, 1957. Before being despatched to the customer the plates are polished. This is to remove dust from bran, which in turn is used to absorb any grease left on the plate. The girl in the photograph is using sheepskin dusters.

Austin Toy Cars, Bargoed, 1951. One of the end products of the tinplate industry is being packed by Oliver Davies of Bargoed and Tom Rees, Gelli-gaer.

Eight

Iron and Steel

Early development of the iron industry in Wales was based on outcrops of iron ore on the northern limits of the South Wales coalfield. The close proximity of coal and limestone to the iron ore enabled extraction of the ore and smelting to take place in the same locality. The addition of limestone to the ore helps to remove acidic impurities such as silica. As explained in the chapter on coal, many pits originally came into being with the intention of servicing the needs of the ironmasters. It was only later that the importance of coal began to outstrip that of iron. It is due to the iron industry that settlements such as Merthyr Tudful, Rhymney, Ebbw Vale, Tredegar, Blaenavon, Hirwaun and Aberdare owe their existence. In Wales the rapid expansion of the iron industry began about 1760 when population growth, increasing industrialisation and wars against the French created greater demand for iron products. Swiftly, once rural communities were transformed into centres of heavy industry attracting thousands of migrant workers from neighbouring areas. By 1801 Merthyr Tudful had a population of 7,700 and was the biggest town in South Wales. By 1825 over £1 million had been invested in the iron industry in the area. A near insatiable demand came into being five years later with the rise of railways in Britain, Europe and North America ensuring that this investment produced a good return.

The peak year for iron production in Wales was in 1857 when over 970,000 tons were produced by 164 furnaces. By this time local supplies were insufficient to meet demand and iron ore was being imported from Spain. From a Welsh point of view a blow to the industry came with the discovery by Henry Bessemer of a method of producing cheap steel in 1856. Although the superiority of steel, which is essentially iron containing half to one and a half per cent carbon, was well known its price prevented it being widely used. The Bessemer process used an egg-shaped converter into which molten iron ore was poured and a stream of air blown upwards, combining with impurities (chiefly carbon, manganese and silica) to be given off as gases or form a crust called slag, which is drawn off. Dowlais was the first British ironworks to adopt the Bessemer process.

Welsh iron ore, however, had a high content of phosphorus causing steel made from it to break easily. As demand for steel grew ironworks had to convert to steel making, concentrate on coal production or close. Those that took the first option were handicapped by the need to transport imported ore low in phosphorus from the docks at Cardiff, Newport or Swansea. This led to some companies re-locating their works in coastal sites near docks. An example of one such company was the Dowlais Company who re-located a large part of their works in East Moors, near Cardiff, earning the plant the nickname of 'New Dowlais'. Production continued on the old site at Dowlais until the eve of the First World War due to the philanthropy of Lord Wimborne, a descendant of the ironmaster John Guest who was concerned about the impact on the local Dowlais community if the company's entire operation was removed.

A rival to Bessemer was the Siemens-Martin or open-hearth process. This was fired not by coal but by coal gas. This relied on two brick-lined chambers containing molten ore. Gases were injected into one chamber, burned on contact with the molten metal and were drawn out from the other, the process being reversed at intervals so that heat from the brick wall of the second chamber could be used to warm the gases being introduced. Open-hearth steel-making used far more fuel than the Bessemer process, took longer but produced a far superior steel as the molten ore was heated to a higher temperature. The longer time taken allowed greater control of the process. Not until 1894 was more steel produced in Britain through the open-hearth process than the Bessemer.

Much work went into developing a process that would enable iron ores high in phosphorus, such as those found in South Wales to be used for steel making. Any solution to the problem hinged on removal of the phosphorus. Despite the wealth of research into the subject it was due to experiments conducted in a shed in Blaenavon by two cousins, Sidney Gilchrist Thomas and Percy Carlyle Gilchrist that the necessary breakthrough was made. Sidney, a court clerk in London and keen amateur metallurgist was the leading light in the partnership. It was his assertion that lining the converter with bricks made from limestone caused the phosphorus to react with the calcium and become absorbed into the slag. His findings gained acceptance in 1879 and revolutionised the industry. In Britain as a whole the invention of this basic process was not regarded with the respect it deserved and allowed Britain's industrial competitors, notably Germany and the USA to dominate the markets.

The steel industry in North Wales was centred on Shotton and Brymbo. It developed from ironworks established in the late seventeenth century at nearby Bersham. The area was favoured by supplies of iron ore, limestone and coal, though in the early days, as in South Wales, charcoal was used as a fuel. Brymbo was developed as an ironworks in the early eighteenth century. The transition to steel production took place in 1885 with the construction of one of the first basic open-hearth furnaces in Britain. With the exception of a break during the depression years of 1931-34 steel making at Brymbo continued until 1990 when closure of the plant was announced.

As a result of the importance of steel to the economy of the country government intervention has played a significant role in dictating the location and running of steel production in Britain. This was achieved principally through nationalisation in 1950 and re-nationalisation in 1967. At the time of writing steel production in Wales is largely concentrated on Shotton, Port Talbot and Llanwern. In January 1995 Llanwern steelworks became the first hot strip mill in Britain to produce over 70,000 tonnes of steel in a week. The tinplate division consists of two sites at Ebbw Vale and Trostre where the loss of nearly 350 jobs was announced due to restructuring in 1994.

The condensers, Dowlais Works, 1906. The three cooling towers or condensers adjacent to Caeharris pond dominate this view of the Dowlais works. The tall chimneys mark the site of the blast furnaces, whilst the cluster of huts on the left of the cooling towers house the silica brickworks. By 1906 the Dowlais Iron Company had been amalgamated into Guest, Keen & Nettlefold, better known as GKN. Much of the production at Dowlais focused on making steel rails which were turned out at the rate of 5,000 tons per week. These were exported to India, Australia, Europe and North America The three cooling towers were demolished in 1937, seven years after an economic downturn caused the closure of the iron and steel-making plants at Dowlais. 3,000 workers lost their jobs as a result. The Big Mill, where the rails were rolled, continued in operation until 1936, when a further 700 workers lost their jobs. Other smaller parts of the complex such as the foundries continued in operation. Construction of the Margam Steelworks at Port Talbot during the early 1950s had a knock-on effect and brought a minor renaissance to the area as a demand for moulds emerged. Later, construction of an engineering complex ensured production of steel products until the 1970s.

The Works, Dowlais, near Merthyr-Tydfil

The Works, Dowlais, near Merthyr Tydfil, *c*. 1905. The circular, dome-shaped towers (centre right) housed three of the blast furnaces at Dowlais. The pipes in the foreground led from the coking ovens.

Brymbo Steel Works.

Brymbo Steel Works, *c*. 1910. At Brymbo the contrast between the heavy industrial nature of steel making and the rural backdrop is nowhere more apparent than in this view. As time progressed and the factory expanded the slag tip advanced to engulf many of the houses on the left and the field on the right. The road underneath the slag tip was re-routed in 1924 with the Brymbo Steel Company picking up most of the cost.

Brymbo steelworkers, 1947. These four workmen are attending one of the electric-arc furnaces installed in 1939. They are wearing safety goggles and steel-toed boots. In addition, two of them have sweat-cloths around their necks to wipe away perspiration. The electric-arc furnaces used scrap metal and supplied high-quality steels to the Air Ministry during the Second World War. They melted the metal by an electric arc drawn between carbon electrodes and did not rely on supplies of coal.

Bessemer plant, Ebbw Vale, *c*. 1905. By the time this postcard was published the Bessemer plant at Ebbw Vale was almost at the end of its working life. In the bottom right two Bessemer converters can be seen. The platform above them was used to load the converters with first scrap and secondly molten iron. The mix was then subjected to a blast of oxygen which combines with the carbon and other impurities which would be dissipated as gases or could be extracted as slag, which was sold to farmers as fertiliser. The process of converting iron to steel took about twenty minutes. The Ebbw Vale works closed in 1929 following a number of indifferent years.

Richard Thomas & Co. Ltd purchased the Ebbw Vale site in 1936 and spent £11 million building the first modern, steel hot-strip mill in Europe. This enabled iron ore entering the blast furnaces to pass through the steel works and on to the rolling mills. Iron ore was imported 150 miles by train from Northamptonshire. The reason to locate the new steel works at Ebbw Vale was primarily a governmental one. It was hoped that the construction of such a plant would alleviate the chronic unemployment situation in the area at the time. In this respect the works was a great success but the awkward location worked against profitability throughout its life. The large integrated steel works at Llanwern near Newport were built in 1960 largely to replace the Ebbw Vale works which now concentrate on galvanising and tin-plating using steel produced at Llanwern.

Casting mill, Ebbw Vale, *c.* 1910. The finished steel ingots can be seen stacked in the bottom of the picture. Before the days of integrated steelworks the ingots would be re-heated in a rolling mill before being rolled into sheets, rails, etc.

Margam steelworks, *c.* 1960. To re-generate steel-making in Britain after 1945 the Steel Development Plan was launched. This included a new integrated works at Margam, near Port Talbot. Like East Moors the site is coastal to enable imported ores to be unloaded directly. Coal and limestone were available nearby and a market for the finished product to be found in tinplate works around Swansea and Llanelli. The chimneys, pipes and storage vessels contrast with the primitive-looking works at Ebbw Vale fifty years earlier.

Victoria blast furnaces, *c.* 1910. The ironworks and collieries at Victoria, two miles south of Ebbw Vale were established in the late 1830s. In 1903 a new, larger blast furnace was built to augment the existing 1882 furnaces. Its design was copied from those in use in American steelworks and was nicknamed 'Yankee'. This is in the centre of the photograph. On the left is the steam engine 'Ariel', one of 25 locomotives used for moving coal, iron ore and finished steel. The blast furnaces in Victoria closed in 1975.

Victoria furnaces, *c.* 1900. In the foreground can be seen the coking ovens where coal from the Victoria collieries was converted to coke before being used in the blast furnaces. The large building on the right is the blast engine house.

Nine

Manufacturing

Like tinplate production much manufacturing industry in Wales during the nineteenth century and first half of the twentieth century was linked to the iron and steel industries, themselves essentially manufacturing industries but one whose considerable importance has made them worthy of consideration in their own right. Additional factors for the location of manufacturing in Wales included the presence of a large workforce conversant with the metal industries, a location near to markets in the Midlands and south-east of England and, by no means least, government aid.

The decades immediately following the Second World War saw manufacturing activity both increase and diversify in South Wales, partly due to the Government Distribution of Industry Policy that encouraged location in the area. One industry to be attracted to the area in this post-war era was motor vehicles. Although assembly of cars was minimal – only Gilbern ever produced cars in Wales – the motor components sector grew to be of some importance. Today the industry still retains a presence through the likes of the Lucas Industries brakes factory and the Ford Engine Plant at Llanelli. At its peak in the mid-1950s the industry employed over 18,000 workers. North Wales was not without its own vehicle components factories such as Ferodo who made brake linings at their factory in Caernarfon, and more recently the Toyota Engine Plant on Deeside, which began production in 1992. A new peak was scaled in 1995 when it was revealed that the motor industry was now the largest manufacturing sector employing over 20,000 people.

The heavy end of the metal industries such as car bodies tended to keep to traditional locations near the steel plants while factories concerned with smaller items such as electrical switches, household utensils and toys tended to find locations further afield. This latter category employed a high proportion of women, often unskilled, employed in production-line assembly work. By 1970 sizeable numbers were employed at engineering works in the coalfield valleys such as EMI at Treorci (750), Aberdare Cables (3,000), AB Metals (3,000) and South Wales Switchgear (2,000).

Between 1974 and 1986 no less than 135,000 jobs in Welsh manufacturing were lost. The decline has been greater amongst women workers, though this has now been partly offset by the number of new opportunities for women workers, many of which are part-time. By 1992 Wales was able to boast nearly 6,000 manufacturing units employing over 230,000 people. The vast majority, over 3,600, were small units employing less than ten persons. Only twenty employed more than one thousand employees. Amongst this category are factories established by Japanese companies which now employ some 13,000 people. Of particular note were the working practices established by these factories. The first Japanese company to invest in Wales was Takiron, who built a factory in Bedwas in 1972. By 1992 there were 29 factories and a number of related activities in operation in Wales. Of these factories the majority (16) are involved with the production of electronic goods such as television sets, video recorders and photocopying machines. The others are involved in the manufacture of chemicals, automotive parts and other precision components. Initially, firms came to Wales merely to assemble imported components into a finished product. As Japanese investment has increased so has the range of activities, with about half the factories now producing components for assembly. This move away from assembly work has also seen a change in the nature of those employed. At first these factories were seen as employing only school-leavers at low rates of pay. But as the nature of activities evolved so did the employment prospects for other sectors.

Factory site in the Rhondda, 1947. This is an example of the type of project developed as part of the Government Distribution of Industry Policy.

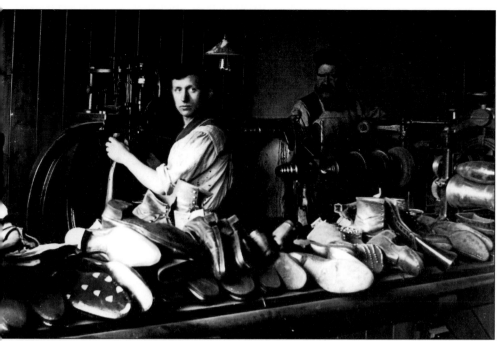

Griffiths Bros. Boot and Shoe Factory, *c.* 1920. One of the most traditional industries in Wales was shoe and boot manufacture. Griffiths Brothers had branches in Llandeilo and Pantyffynnon, the latter concerned mostly with selling boots to the colliers.

Midland Metal Spinners, Neath, 1955. Coming off the production line are teapots made from locally produced tinplate.

Limes Brothers Toy Factory, Merthyr Tudful, 1951. Two staff carefully check and pack the finished product ready for the Christmas rush.

Harrison's Welsh Toffee, 1959. Established in Penrhyndeudraeth, Harrison's Welsh toffee was popular in many parts of the British Empire.

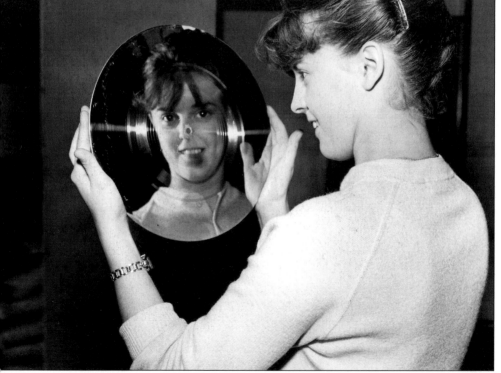

Qualiton Records, 1959. Based in Pontardawe, Qualiton produced a wide range of records in English and Welsh. Employee Gillian Williams is seen here inspecting a master disc from which records will be pressed.

Ferranti, Bangor, 1959. It was not until the 1950s that many remoter part of Wales received electricity for the first time. Ferranti in Bangor specialised in making electricity meters, here being checked before despatch.

St Margaret's Clothes Factory, Aberbargoed, 1951. Textile works traditionally rely on women workers, usually in relatively low-paid jobs.

Places To Visit

Big Pit Mining Museum, Blaenafon
(Tel: 01495 790311)
Museum of a typical coal mine both above and below ground. Open March-December.

Blaenavon Ironworks
(Tel: 01495 552036)
Situated near Big Pit, it was at this site that experiments were perfected that gave rise to the Gilchrist-Thomas Bessemer process. Open April-September.

Bryn Tail Lead Mine, Llanidloes
(Tel: 01222 465511)
Open-air museum on the site of a nineteenth-century lead mine. Open all year.

Brynkir Woollen Mill, Porthmadog
(Tel: 01766 75236)
Working woollen mill with exhibitions of processes involved and the opportunity to purchase goods made at the factory. Open all year.

Cefn Coed Colliery Museum, Crynant
(Tel: 01639 750556)
Situated in surface buildings close to Blaenant Colliery, this attraction offers displays of machinery, a mock-up of a mining gallery and a nature trail. Open April-October.

Gloddfa Ganol Slate Mine, Blaenau Ffestiniog
(Tel: 01766 830664)
A working slate mine, visitors can have a guided tour of underground workings as well as examining the mills were slate is split. Miners' cottages have been renovated to show life in different decades during the present and last centuries. Open April-September.

Llechwedd Slate Caverns, Blaenau Ffestiniog
(Tel: 01766 830306)
An underground railway takes visitors around the workings where audio-visual resources are used to illustrate the history of the complex. Above ground visitors can watch slate splitters at work or visit Victorian-style shops. Open all year.

Llywernog Silver-Lead Mining Museum, Ponterwyd
(Tel: 01970 85620)
Six and a half acre site chronicling the mining of silver and lead in Ceredigion. Some underground workings open to the public. Open April-September.

Museum of the Welsh Woollen Industry, Drefach Felindre
(Tel: 01559 370929)
Museum has an exhibition charting the history of the industry from the Middle Ages. Open all year.

Porthmadog Maritime Museum
(Tel 01766 513736)
Quayside museum with emphasis on shipping and the local slate trade on which the shipping depended. Open April-September.

Swansea Maritime and Industrial Museum
(Tel: 01792 650351)
Situated adjacent to the marina on the site of the city's docks, this museum has an impressive collection of vintage vehicles, boats and locomotives. Open all year.

Welsh Industrial & Maritime Museum, Cardiff
(Tel: 01222 481919)
Large museum with exhibits and displays chronicling the industrial and maritime heritage of the principality. Open all year.

Big Pit, *c*. 1994, Mike Read, colliery official, leads visitors along a roadway 100m underground. (Reproduced courtesy of Big Pit).

Bibliography

Birch, A. and Cass, F., *The Economic History of the British Iron & Steel Industry* (1967)

Brynkir Woollen Mill, *Brynkir Woollen Mill* (1973)

Coal's New Face (NCB Publications, n.d.)

Davies, Conway, *The Coal Industry in Wales* (WHRU, 1985)

Egan, David, *Coal Society* (Gomer Press, 1987)

Elis-Williams, M, *Packet to Ireland*

George, K.D. and Mainwaring, L., *The Welsh Economy* (UWP, 1988)

Glover, Brian, *Prince of Ales* (Alan Sutton Publishing, 1993)

Hughes, D. Lloyd & Williams, Dorothy M., *Holyhead, the Story of a Port* (1967)

Hughes, Simon, *The Cwmystwyth Mines* (NMRS, 1981)

Jenkins, J. Geraint, *The Welsh Woollen Industry* (National Museum of Wales, 1969)

Jenkins, J. Geraint, *Coracles and Nets* (David & Charles, 1974)

Jenkins, J. Geraint, *Inshore Fishermen of Wales* (UWP 1991)

Jones, D. Ioan, *Brymbo Steel Works, a collection of pictures* (Bridge Books, 1991)

Jones, I.W., *Slate and Slatemen of Llechwedd* (Quarry Tours Ltd, 1975)

Lawrence, Roy, *A Directory of the South Wales Coalfield* (RAL Promotions, 1987)

Lewis, W.J., *Lead Mining in Wales* (UWP, 1967)

Lieven, Michael, *Senghenydd. The Universal Pit Village* (Gomer Press, 1994)

Lindsay, Jean, *A History of the North Wales Slate Industry* (David & Charles, 1974)

Lloyd, W.J.H., *Fishing boats of Tenby* (Mariners Mirror, Vol. 44)

Luxton, Brian, *Old Barry in Photographs Vols. 1 & 3* (Stewart Williams)

Morris, E.R., *A Pictorial Survey of Llanidloes* (Powysland Club, 1988)

Morris, J., et al, *Working for the Japanese* (Athlone Press, 1993)

Pounds, N.J.G., *The Geography of Iron & Steel* (Hutchison University Library, 1959)

Rees, D. Morgan, *Industrial Archaeology of Wales* (1975)

Richards Maurice, *Newtown in Old Picture Postcards* (European Library, 1985)

Thomas, W.G., *Welsh Coal Mines* (Amgueddfa Genedlaethol Cymru, 1977)

Vaizey, John, *The History of British Steel* (Weidenfield & Nicholson, 1974)

Williams, Glanmor, (ed.) *Swansea, An Illustrated History* (1990)

Williams, Merfyn, *The Slate Industry* (Shire Publications, 1991)

Opener, Clayton tinplate works, 1957. To prevent the steel sticking together after flattening into plates it had to be prised apart. Despite being a heavy and demanding job it was usually the preserve of women. The dangerous nature of the work required that the arms be protected as well as boots and apron worn.